Proud
  Words
    On
      A
        Dusty
          Shelf

MODERN PRINTING COMPANY
Toledo, Ohio

Copyright ® 1990 by David G. Bick
All rights reserved. No part of this work
may be reproduced or transmitted in any form,
electronic or mechanical, including photocopying
or recorded except as may be expressly permitted
by the 1976 Copyright Act or in writing from the publisher.
Requests for such permission should be addressed to:

The Modern Printing Company
954 Phillips Avenue
Toledo, Ohio 43612

ISBN 0-9625775-0-2

To my children...poetry in motion
Jennifer, Jesse, Matthew & Wylie

Special thanks to all those who have helped make this book a reality and for those who helped in the editing and criticism process. They include Laura Duym, Denise Gallagher, Amy Kaintz, Kory Kaintz, Jodi Kuyper, Marilyn London, Jon Mininger, Maggie Sallah, Tom Sandercock, Beth Stutz and Erin Sullivan.

Also, special thanks to **Glenn Frey, Don Henley, Janis Ian, Billy Joel** and **Billy Vera** for the use of their songs in this book and for their encouragement and support.

Thank you Patricia Ryan-Rogers for putting up with all the retypes, drafts and constant changes in the process of preparing this manuscript.

Table of Contents

I. **I'VE LOVED THESE DAYS — BILLY JOEL** 1
   - Gypsies Warning 2
   - Easy Decision 3
   - Subtle Remains 4
   - Gridlock 5
   - Fallen Angels 6
   - Tug of War 7
   - Other Euphemisms for Love 8
   - Actor Out of Role 9
   - Illustrations 10
   - Lunch Hour 11
   - Meeting 12
   - One Nighter 13
   - Scavenger Hunt 14
   - Variety and Spice 15
   - Missing Chances 16
   - No Rules 18
   - Moving Day 19
   - Ignorance is Bliss 20
   - Northeasterly 21
   - Lovers & Other Strangers 22
   - Heads and Tails 23
   - Penny Candy 24
   - Honeymoon 25
   - Invitation 26
   - Pendant 27
   - Perfect Woman 28
   - A Toast to Clearasil 29
   - Hell 30
   - Short Dance to a Long Song 31

II. **BETWEEN LIKE AND LOVE — BILLY VERA** 32
   - Photographic 33
   - The One That Got Away 34
   - Together 35
   - Ticking Clock 36
   - Just as Expected 38
   - Sabbatical 39
   - Intentions 40
   - The Goddess 41
   - Portrait 42
   - Steamy Windows 43
   - Masking Faces 44

Words Hurt	45
It's a Matter of Time	46
Split Personality	47
A Tribute to Rap Music	48
Short Introduction	49
First Lover	50
I'm the Dancer	51
Romantic	52
What You Want to Hear	53
I Dance Too	54
Dawn	55
Practices and Partners	56
Gravity	57
Intro to Life 101	58
Virgin	59

III. AFTER THE THRILL IS GONE — GLENN FREY & DON HENLEY ... 60

Paupers and Profiteers	61
Torch Song	62
Nothing's Changed	63
Exorcism	64
Notes to Myself	65
The Walk	66
Passing Years	67
Carpe Diem	68
Surrender	69
Phone Calls	70
Graceful Deceit	72
First Impressions	73
The Misinformed, Lovers and the Heartbroken	74
Lost Kiss	76
Tables Turned	77
Wholesale	78
Postage Due	79
Doors Have Knobs on Both Sides	80
Is the Pope Catholic?	81
Words and Music By...	82
Birthday Girl	83

IV. BETWEEN THE LINES — JANIS IAN ... 84

Sports Heroes and Cheerios	86
In the Stretch	87
Tribute to Rod McKuen	88
Gift	89
Geneology	90
Two Trees Only Grow...	92

Road Pizza	93
Magic	94
The Home	95
Cheerleader	96
Slaughterhouse	97
Love's Labor	98
Time	100
Conception	102
Today	104
Sounds of Love	105
Higher Education	106
Old What's Her Name	107
The Contributions of Disco Music	108
Second Wind	109
Court & Spark	110
Sundays are for Suicide	111
Santa's Lap	112
Waking the Dead	114
Nature's Way	115
Roll the Dice	116
Once Upon a Time	118
Contradictions — The Last Poem	119

I've Loved These Days

Now we take our time . . . so nonchalant,
And spend our nights so bon vivant.
We dress our days in silken robes,
The money comes, the money goes . . .
We know it's all a passing phase.
We light our lamps for atmosphere
And hang our hopes on chandeliers.
We're going wrong, we're gaining weight,
We're sleeping long and far too late.
And so it's time to change our ways . . .
But I've loved these days.
Now as we indulge in things refined,
We hide our hearts from harder times.
A string of pearls, a foreign car . . .
Oh, we can only go so far . . .
on caviar and Cabernet.
We drown our doubts in dry champagne,
And soothe our souls with fine cocaine.
I don't know why I even care . . .
We get so high and get nowhere.
We'll have to change our jaded ways . . .
But I've loved these days.
So before we end (and then begin)—
We'll drink a toast to how it's been . . .
A few more hours to be complete,
A few more nights on satin sheets,
A few more times that I can say . . .
I've loved these days.

I'VE LOVED THESE DAYS — Copyright, Home Grown Music and Tin Pan Tunes. From the album TURNSTILES written and performed by Billy Joel. Reprinted here with kind permission of Billy Joel. I appreciate your help, buddy!

Gypsy's Warning

(This handwritten poem was discovered in family archives while researching genealogy.)

Trust him not O, gentle lady
though his voice be low and sweet.
Heed not him who kneels before thee
softly pleading at thy feet.
Now thy life is in its morning,
cloud not this thy happy lot,
listen to the gypsy's warning
gentle lady trust him not.

Lady, once there lived a maiden,
young and loose and like thee fair,
yet he wooed he wooed and won her,
thrilled her gentle heart with care;
then he heeded not her weeping,
he cared not her life to save.
Soon she perished, now she is sleeping
in the cold and silent grave.

Lady turn not from me so coldly,
for I have only told the truth
from a stern and withering sorrow.
Lady I would shield thy youth,
I would shield thee from all danger,
shield thee from a tempest's snare.
Lady shun the dark eyed stranger
I have warned thee now beware.

Take your gold I do not want it,
Lady I have prayed for this,
for the hour that I might foil him
and rob him of expected bliss.
Aye! I see thou art filled without warning
at my look so fierce and wild.
Lady in the churchyard yonder,
sleeps the Gypsy's only child.

Easy Decision

You're not the architect of love
or the genius behind the passion,
for your heart's a bit cold
and your hand a bit too practiced.
Get away from me now,
I know that look and it could seduce the devil.
Yes, your lips are responsive
and your body ready to be explored,
but already your head is calculating
seventeen roads to fantasy.
Your eyes have a look of evil—
I'm not to be devoured by your greed.
It's time to return to my fantasy lover,
one that never betrays me,
feeds me the lies easy to believe
and visions of what to be.
So let me down one more time
by now it's no disgrace.
Back to my crystal ball lover
where I put on a fanciful display
of clever retorts and sweet nothings,
philosophy that won't get laughed at, you know,
nothing to puncture my pride.
So let me return to my invisible lover,
for never hurting my sense of worth
is better than being slain for your personal gain.

Subtle Remains

Hair still clinging to the side of the sink,
towel hanging crooked on the rack,
even the perfume smell of yesterday
rallies the scent to my nostrils.
The bed lingers still of your outline
and that smell which only lovers leave when
they move on to unknown places.
How long this time? How long till the
unknown becomes the known, till the past
scurries to catch that
already gone, departed so hurriedly?
"When the spirit moves," or something like that,
God! Even phrases hang in the air it is so thick.
It is stale indeed, its presence
more rancid with love filled nights and half
missed kisses that fled from mouth to mouth;
wrecked sheets and strewn blankets lining the
path of the last adventure.
Now I find myself musing as if this just a phase,
another pressing time when fruit ripens
and disappears before its freshness decays.
Ripe? Maybe, but this tree still blossoms
waiting the gardener's delicate touch.
There is no solace in subtle remains,
no memory harder than those lost in vain.
How wicked a revenge these whirlwind ladies conceive
when a one room life is their legacy.

Gridlock

Does the weight of my stare
disturb you in these otherwise quiet moments?
At times like these I memorize the curl of your hair,
gold on your neck and the corner of your mouth.
I enjoy these moments and steal some part of what
you would normally hide
and wonder about likes and habits.
It seems like we've known each other forever,
the children, school, work and the rest of daily living.
It seems like we've been here forever.
The radio plays a song from last year,
your lips in sync with the lyric and you
apply some color to your lips,
our eyes then catch sight of another,
I lean as if to replace that strand of hair,
you notice my look, grimace, grab your wheel,
destroying the moment and we both move on
to see what the next red light has in store.

Fallen Angel

"Destiny is not a matter of chance,
it is a matter of choice,
it is not a thing
to be waited for,
it is a thing to be achieved."

William Jennings Bryan

Some of them were as promiscuous as money,
some scholars in the art of being lonely,
Ph.D.'s in deceiving themselves and oft times others.
They betrayed themselves often,
afraid the "coy mistress" would never have her day.
What I provoked beneath the prim and proper
all-American everything with the swimmer's tan
was lurking there already in their mind's eye.
In my whims they deserve something of merit,
becoming disciples committing heinous crimes
as loving before marriage
lacking intent of the carriage.
It is for you that I give my hagiographic listing,
you who "gather rosebuds" while in your splendor.
And yes, I took you but you taught me to be tender,
to give my unconditional surrender,
became the ultimate pretender, if you please,
to enjoy the rhapsody with thee.
Even the sun sets daily I said—"carpe diem"
and you agreed,
tumbling and searching we did for ecstasy,
bedroom olympics, our own brand of immortality.
You never worried about little things
and in this lesson I learned never to argue details
and the value of anger.
So I dedicate this to you Fallen Angels, one and all.
I grieve not because you've deprived me of pleasure
but because you've been so long removed,
God, I miss your measure!
Our destiny was not chance but choice.
It was not to be waited for
and we plucked it like a plum,
both hungry to seize the fruit
and sharing each other's loot.

Tug of War

Ah, who is right?
If I had come to you vulnerable,
would you have loved me?
Had you loved me,
would I have become strong?
The question bellows:
    Who hurts more?
    Who loves more?
A contest for the unworthy,
the prize is fault.
And now our mood is stuttering between
the hostile wall of our hurts
and between the soft moans and purrs.
Your words were hurled like weapons
and I too tired to carry another shield.
We are now sharing
that bittersweet process
of putting and pushing arguments
and deciding which of us
will be privileged
enough to feel
the greater
guilt.

Other Euphemisms For Love

"A double . . . whatever for the
crazy ladies that visited
my past, ladies now a vintage
memory in the corner of my head."

"A triple . . . whatever the lady
is drinking — she deserves it
bartend — she's a girl from my
hectic, horny days of yesterday!"

Sometimes they haunt me
into beckoning the madness back
from where I had them stored.
I don't know how they appear
and disappear like some kind of magic act.
Ah, yes, they are remnants
from chest-pounding interludes of my
dementia youth now serving
as bedtime fables when I sleep.
She, like the others left before the dawn,
but her perfume's still the same
and she said I left her bruised
and hurt . . . but I doubt it.
Some of them actually cared,
at least they said as much.
Maybe they cared as much as
they could, which is why I can't seem to remember.

"Let's pour another round
for the zany apparitions that
reappear periodically.
'Pass the double, bartend',"
for all those mental midgets
infected with moronic plague
who gave me midnight tricks wrapped in
laughter and giggling in the dark.
They are the remains, my personal
historians, who can tell me what
I used to be and maybe a little of why.

Actor Out Of Role

What you see
are my invented masks,
collected images of
self-protection.
Reality is whatever
you would have me be.
I lurk somewhere inside,
saving myself for those
who bother to ask.
My door opens
from your side only.
A protection, I suppose,
that rewards lovers
and lets passers-by
pass by.
Turn the knob
whenever you choose
and pray you find
the creator as worthy
as his creations.

Illustrations

"If this the face that launched the ships,
Lean gently from thy tower.
Loose from thy lips one gentle kiss
Granting immortal power."

Your sleep is that of a newborn,
a vision of honesty that penetrates
more than your eyes so well trained.
To keep you young
I will freeze this moment and relish it
even when our words refuse to obey
the heart and the speech somewhere inside.

You look funny asleep with your mouth half-cocked
and your crooked smile—amusing.
My foolishness during these moments
lacks in its customary pretense.
To keep you lusty and my fantasies alive
I will plan tomorrows so you won't see
my plan, keeping the future an adventure
where I will give you love
and not love love and its absurdities.

I will keep you like this
though no doubt we will change,
glimpses stolen in odd hours to
see you best in unseen situations
and laugh softly when I know you
have no protection.
I will keep you like this
to help you become my dreams,
forcing you to love yourself
as much as I do when you sleep.

Lunch Hour

There is a clock outside my window
that tells me what the day is like.
Yesterday it said to leave my coat,
get a turkey, mayo and cheese on a bun,
a cold Diet Coke and dine in the park.
So I did.
And watched as the birds circled
and the pretty girls chasing forty minute lunch hours
and nibbled on my turkey, mayo and cheese and
sipped my Diet Coke.
I was taken by the girl with the freckles
that moved to her shoulders and into her striped top . . .
the sway of her hair . . .
and forgot all about whatever moot
point it was we couldn't resolve the night before.
Then it occurred to me that
I was going to fall in love with someone
new again next Wednesday at the latest.
Can you blame me?
All it cost me this time is the price
of a turkey, mayo and cheese
and one more Diet Coke.

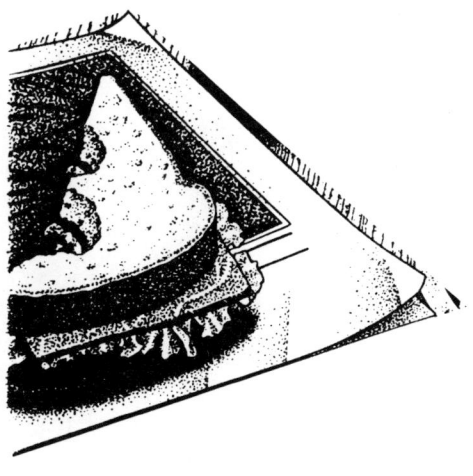

Meeting

I met a beautiful girl today.
She made me funny, funnier
than I really am so she would laugh.
She made me handsome
so she could gaze at me.
She made me honest
so she could believe me.
She made me sensitive
so I could understand her pain.
She has made me everything
she needs to survive tonight.
She has taken me off the rack
and made me fit perfect without alteration.
And I am glad of it,
for I can delight in me again.
She must survive tonight
so we can begin tomorrow together.
And I am glad of it,
for I can delight in me again
and begin to marvel her.

One Nighter

I don't care if your name be
Jan or Lynn or Sue —
If you go or went to school.
Don't give me the name
of your favorite book or movie,
not even the interest can be faked.
Say instead that I look strong
and have a distinctive smile,
that you're attracted to me
because our eyes speak the same idiom.
Move instead out of the actress role,
dispense with silly protocol
that neither of us believe.
Move as if you meant this,
let your touch talk of silent things.
Your movements convey more than a shadow
strolling across the backdrop of the room.
We'll feel better even with the
knowledge that we will steal from here
before dawn and our time not forgotten,
caress and messy sheet remembered along
with wet kisses, for we'll take a vow not
to measure responses or compare notes
on others who took this same liberty with us.
Being accustomed to another
means passion turned to practice
and more fantasies than government programs.
So when the door creaks open
and reality appears in cameo,
pretend you're not looking Joan, Nancy or Jo,
and I'll remember you more than the emptiness
of any single day,
more than the feeling of a dream
that never had its way.

Scavenger Hunt

It started at breakfast.
she offered me a face
I didn't know she owned
and became a new lover.
So I gave her something
new of mine
and she repaid me with
a giggle I had never heard.
We read the newspaper
to each other, bartering thoughts,
finding within ourselves new jokes.
She turned her head
and I noticed a new curve
in a neck I'd explored forever
the night before.
I am awaiting next weekend
to find what adventures it brings
and what new pieces of the puzzle will be discovered.

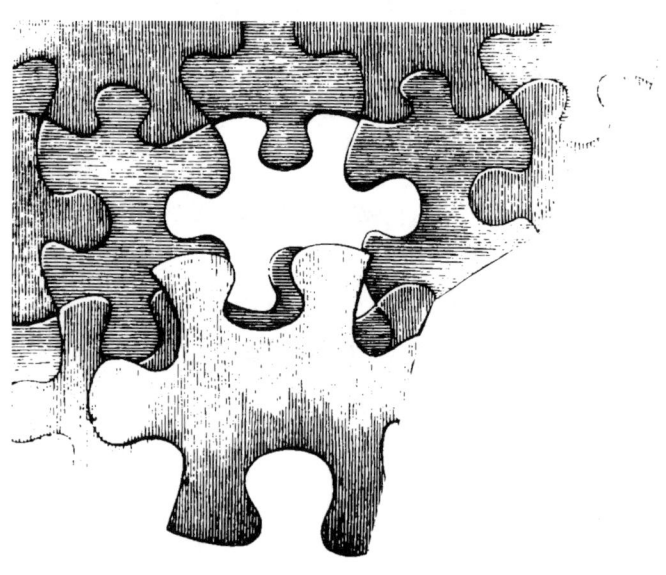

Variety and Spice

Permit me my zaniness lady
and my obvious lack of cultivation.
My frenzy has been certified,
so pardon my inept clumsiness
when I begin my seduction.
Instead, show me your eccentric ways
and play yourself in character,
unafraid of performing for this audience of one.
There will be no parades to welcome
our coming, only the heavy air
that rushes our lungs reminding us
of the prize for prurient indulgences.
Bow to my ridiculous tics lady,
and rejoice with me in this assault,
in the tickle of the sweat that creates
a map down our foreheads,
salute the crashing of the hearts
in our chests, for soon we must return
to normalcy and learn to act within
the bounds maturity has established for us.
So, please permit me my temporary
leave of absence and enjoy your residence in
my personal lunatic fringe.

Missing Chances (Sandy)

I am searching for a memory
because there is something quite vain in me
that won't let sleeping dogs lie
or let bygones be bygones and because
I remember too much of you and things
that could have been if our timing had been better.
Somewhere in time,
time could have been much kinder.

There is still time I suppose
but then we never really worried about telling time.
Now you are taken,
taken as much as I was taken by you,
but years bury feelings and memories
but somewhere in time I hope to excavate
feelings pent up in the past.

I thought about you last week when I
passed the building by the zoo where you once lived.
I didn't need to awaken any memory about how we
shared our youth in the anonymous dark,
scampered off to work and
felt guilty of trickery, even if our thoughts
were only for each other.

We have missed each other too many times
and I have shared in absentia
the past, present and future
that never really happened because our clocks
were never set to alert us to the moment.
I am so sure of so little lately
except that somewhere in time in that building
part of you remains with me
and some day I hope to find the right door
before it is too late.

No Rules

Come,
let me tell you lies
and map your white body
with eyes that have traveled
too many times to this destination.
Please,
follow me into worlds
where no language is understood
except that unspoken,
silence the rule which endures.
Come, please,
into this place where
what you find is the only truth
worth trying to attain,
where love is what you want it to be,
all, of course, depending on your need.
Don't fret the past you hold with disdain
in this world without rules,
no games to start and end,
the end and beginning only that
you choose — come with me and
know you may not win,
but neither will you lose.

Moving Day

I'm down, lady.
It's time I left.
Long ago I stopped
believing your dreams
and a moment ago
I promised us a future
and laughed in my own face.

We have all the symptoms:
Suspicion, fear
and the trembling dread
of going out there
once more to search
among the faces
for another disappointment.

I'm down, lady,
but I'll prevail.
My history guarantees it.
I will outlast this anguish
to learn another face,
explore another contour,
so I can offer her
all those rare presents
you should have opened
in person.

Ignorance Is Bliss

The less said about my slut the better.
Nobody knows how or who or why I met her,
with her waterfall colored hair
and dainty pointed feet,
but what a way to exercise with her,
so willing is she to keep fit
as a matter of regimen, not burden.

A little whiskey improves her lies,
a little dark makes deep her eyes,
a little chill in the air refines her touch,
and when we're alone her tongue is sweet and such.

When evenings come I begin my summer classes
I spread out with the slut
and begin my formal education,
stare at the powder caked on her face
and kiss the slut all over the place.

Bliss is nice, this ignorance,
but a little bit will do.
I've had too much and so's the slut too.
To see the prints of time in her eyes,
hear her moaning sure makes a boy wise.

Northeasterly

This morning I found your picture,
a souvenir of sorts like the unmade bed
at noontime; fitting I suppose,
for you were always one for cashing in
dreams for small fortunes as opposed to
seeking long term dividends only afforded
those on nine hour schedules.
Really, I don't need to recall much
about the way you squeezed toothpaste
from the middle and always left the
toilet paper empty (occasionally still
angry thinking of those awkward times).
It is always the morning after like this
that time loses its hands, deja vu
a somewhat constant companion.
Sometimes years later you still feel
no relief, perhaps none is wanted.
Oh, your smell has gone now,
the windows have carried your scent
to another's side, time aired itself.
Yet the bed still remains unmade,
sheets wrinkled, waiting, I hope, for
the wind to change direction.

Lovers and Other Strangers

It's no wonder
each of us fail together.
Given the fact that our talk
and time is devoted to accumulating
bigger and better
houses
washers
dryers
warm vacations in summer
and cold scenery come winter.
Not once did we speak of the time
spent silently sitting together
or about the price tag of trust.
Time is now measured by money possessed,
not that we would or wouldn't
rather spend time together
instead of spending idle chatter with pseudo friends
whose latest
LCD
Digital
Laser
Big Picture do all everything
gains more of your attention
than staying late in bed with me
forgetting the trash and dusting anytime today,
perhaps even listening to some inane thing I might say.
Your eyes could see but didn't understand,
sometimes you listened but never did you learn.
Maybe that's why it's said that
when dreams die they don't whimper, they scream.
It's the only way they're heard.

Heads and Tails

I'm crazy, a loner,
selfish and lazy?
That's what you say.
Speak it if you feel
you must but it is your tone
to which I object.
If I threaten you, then
leave the room and lock
the door if you must,
feel safe in your isolation.
Take with you the victory
on your way out — the last word.
Take with you your anger,
admonish my ways and means.
It is difficult to be sorry
when I'm not in the least.
Hell, I'm no hypocrite!
It is I who is offended!
Yes, because I see differently
and take solace in myself,
and believe in these beer glass eyes
some of the best company I have yet to find.
If I am all you think,
I refuse to share my misery
and bring you into that hole.
Empathy is still no crime,
you will still not be the Beauty
and I no less the Beast.
I make no promise to where we're going
only promise that we are going on.
How do you ever expect to see the rainbow
if you can't stand a little drizzle?

Penny Candy

Come smiling
gently, gently
offering lies.
Play softly, play
beautifully the
music of the gods.
Speak sweetly muse,
speak ever so wisely.
Steal kisses like
penny candy and talk
of wishes quite tender
and somewhat true.
Steal my heart silently,
quietly as if I weren't there.
Believe my lies offering
your wise experience in return,
playing to our mutual disguise.

Honeymoon

I wrap around you
like a sponge and
soak within your
every secretion.
I will continue to
absorb all that is
given until each pore
cries with fullness.
Then, having achieved
my usefulness,
like a parasite I will
excuse, divorce myself
from your table and roll with the
dancing tides onward
to new experiences.

Invitation

Let us scamper now
toward a shared mischief.
Your quick laughs
have already told me
that I will squeeze you
and kiss you wetly
while I explore
the contours of your nape.
I'll awake and find you
asleep, beside me,
warm in my bed.
So follow me now.
Let me memorize
with a scholarly mouth
the cadence of your body,
and pause to taste your sweetness.
Share this mischief with me
for some brief moments.
I can promise you
an instant of possession;
a single cry of surrender
to echo forever,
a legacy of delight.

Pendant

Your tongue explores
your upper lip
in a gesture
at once erotic,
at once innocent,
and your admission price
is paid for one more evening.
My moods are fed by
that magic fuel of yours.
I wear you around my neck,
a magic charm
to frighten away boredom.
I stumble along,
falling behind
in this giddy race
to capture with open legs
all the technicolor experiences
of a lifetime.
I shut off your music
to freeze your dancing body
and your eyes tell me
that you offer the world,
your moist gifts
only to pass the time
while you stroke your pendant
awaiting the zenith, forgetting the nadir,
anticipating the denouement.

Perfect Woman

(Every man alive
Will live and die
Searching for his perfect woman.)

The luscious woman of imagination
Has a throat round as the pillars
That supported Rome.

The immaculate woman of perfection
Has long full straight hair
Running, bouncing over her body.

This passionate creature of intoxication
Supple limbs bony and discreet,
Sways in gentle motion
Like trees in the April wind.

The lustful madness,
Her eyes that shine in daylight,
Reflect a certain glee
In the twinkling of twilight.

Her texture bronzed
Like statues tanned
By the gentle scorching of the sun.

The perfect woman
Slender, brisk and innocent
Is the walking hand in hand
Of nature's image
Dancing in our eyes.

A Toast to Clearasil

I drink to
your total absence of soul.
Perfect you are,
not stirred even by passion.
You crush the bystanders
in your plotted journey
toward today's pleasure.
You have made greed an art.
I'm no stranger to love but
with you hurt has been more faithful
and I'm not paying any more interest
on a debt I never owed.
You have made yourself available to others
willing to pay the price
simply because fidelity would probably
make your skin break out.

Hell

There were good times
and of course the bad,
but nobody promised any different.
Besides, it made a Christian out of me.
Really it did,
because now that I have been
through hell, I know that there's a heaven.
What bothered me throughout the
trip through hell was the disturbing fact
that you fluently spoke the language.

Short Dance to a Long Song

I am losing you again
as if you were ever mine to lose.
The frivolity would be exciting if
it wasn't for the situation.
You entered my world somehow
with your quiet laugh when my anger in general
was like thunder day and night.
You disarmed me somehow and I felt things
that I thought had died.
The frenzy of phone talk and the
rising pulse when you looked coy
only fueled my nervousness.
I was like a child again and unafraid
until you reacted to the situation
and exited as quickly as you entered.
Now I'm not sure if I'm worried more
about the hurt you left me with
or the hurt you inflicted on yourself.

Between Like and Love

Oh I wish there was a word to describe
The way I feel for you when you're holding me tight
When we're locked in a sweet embrace
And you touch me on my face
I wish there was a word for the way I feel

Love is something I once knew before
But she threw it all away when she walked out the door
And what I'm feeling now
Is something quite apart
I'm lost somewhere between like and love

Somewhere between like and love
Much more than one not quite the other
How can we know if we run and hide
Somewhere between like and love

It makes me happy just to be with you
But I'm afraid to start loving you

And sometimes when you've gone off in the morning
I can smell your sweet perfume where we slept
In the night

Like a promise without words
Often felt but never heard
Makes me almost believe in love again

Somewhere between like and love
Much more than one not quite the other
How can we know if we run and hide
Somewhere between like and love

BETWEEN LIKE AND LOVE — Copyright, WB Music Corp./Vera Cruz Music Company. Written and Performed by Billy Vera on the album RETRONUEVO. Billy, thanks for your songs, old and new!

Photographic (Chris)

I am not nearly as pleased with myself
as I am with the quality of the film still in my head.
It has kept you in better condition than I,
no memory except that which is exposed.
Had I thought more clearly then
things would have found their way to change
but time has no meaning at twenty-one when
you'll live forever and plans are made
only as far ahead as next Tuesday.
I still worry about the ones like you,
the ones I never made love to,
and worry more about than most of those that I did.
I wonder if your uncle survived the stroke,
if grandmother was ever cured,
if the Fourth of July still makes you smile
if you found a way to make a down payment
for the home you desired so.
Did someone find you in time?
I still worry about you
the one I never made love to, but did.

The One That Got Away

I must be satisfied with stolen glances
and your company at occasional social events
because I have no choice.
After phone calls I think about how to
shave ten years off my face or how to age you faster,
like one of those math puzzles
in story problem form
that I never learned to correctly solve,
but then again, it changes nothing.
Perhaps the best hair that money can buy . . . no,
it is not my way to be a little less of anything.
The clock stops for no one and makes cowards of us all.
Yet when I glance in the mirror
I see a young boy looking back at me.
Time is anesthesia for the reflected change.

I must be satisfied with antiseptic feelings
at gatherings of innocent acclaim,
no mingling in private or soft words in bed,
no fantasy of trickling sweat on
those humid August nights, so I turn my head
when images overtake me.
Still I think about the fervor of your dancing tongue
when I turn out the lights.

Still I must be satisfied, because I would rather have this
and only this than to tell you this
and risk losing even the fantasy
and occasional brush of your touch.
I hope and have prayed for the would's and could's
but settled for maybe's and cannot's.
For if I break the rules of the game
I'd be twice as sorry and you'd be just as gone.

Together

You have opened me up
like a clenched fist,
stretching the tendons
of my mistrust
a finger at a time
so I can feel you better
and trust you more.

You have let me like myself
enough to listen at times.
I once used to only
gather my thoughts
and prepare my defenses,
so I could be a safe place
invulnerable to surprise.

You have cured me of my wanderings,
freeing me of the fiction
of power and possession,
making of you a friend
so I ride you only
with your shared consent.

You have declined the credit
and left unopened the
presents of my gratitude.
Once again my instincts
make you logical to me,
for your once spontaneous passion
has now become a sophisticated exercise
holding me hostage
and guarding youth in a safe haven
from the realities of tomorrow.

Ticking Clock

We are yellowing now.
The edges of love
are beginning to curl
while you talk of yesterdays,
opening dusty drawers of hate.
All hope has left your eyes
so you search mine
looking for a sign.
The strain is showing now.
It is tenuous, each step must be carefully measured.
Each word, each phrase jealously spoken for already
there are too many words hanging in the room.
There is no one to see.
I am still here,
still listening.
But I am finishing
my can of Diet Coke
and I will light
one more cigarette.
I will nod for you,
look sad for you,
but I will soon drain my pop,
crush my Viceroy,
and leave you
to seek the answer
without me.
You can talk
of reasons and yesterdays
to an empty glass
and the still warm
hollow cushion
on your chair.
There will only be the
thunderous silence of the ticking clock
swallowing all sound in the room.
Too many times you rehearsed leaving
but this time I'll not look around.

Just As Expected

God, you were perfect!
A smooth, white,
sweet smelling child.
You came to me
without stories
without history,
bearing no scars.
You were a gift
for those who seek
reasons to survive.

You frightened me then.
you were too much
to deserve
until I probed and discovered
that one small
angry speck
in the middle
of your soul
that you pried and picked
until you became
one of us, blemished
and stripped of innocence.

Sabbatical

I'm back, ladies!
How has the party
gone without me?

I told you
I was gone for good,
but I lied.

I've been living
in the upstairs bedroom
enjoying another disaster.

I'm back ladies,
to please you all again—
given the time.

I'm between tragedies
searching for future disappointments
so come forward now
for a brief moment
while I sort you out
in neat stacks of
almosts, could-have-beens
and near-misses.

Intentions

So many things I meant to say.
To please, to praise, to make you glad,
Such splendid chances have I had.
And yet I let them slip away;
And now in shame I bow my head
For moments lost, for words unsaid.

So many deeds I planned to do
To ease the road of your quest.
But while I loitered taking rest,
Another hand has bested mine.
Now my heart is pierced with pain,
For empty actions wrecked in vain.

So many songs I meant to sing
To spur you to greater heights.
To sing, to cheer on lonely nights
When confidence is weak.
But while I tarried with my song,
Your struggling soul grew strong.

Without my words you reached your goal,
Without my help you choose your course.
I need your songs and your deeds,
For now my path is rough.
So I bow my head for moments lost
And for the words unsaid.

The Goddess (For Laura)

Solemn face
unsmiling, brown hair
cascading, hugging beautifully
those stately shoulders.

Feminine finger nimbly rests
upon her gentle nose, a flick
of the wrist and her hair parts
disclosing a pair of saddle brown
eyes matching her buoyant hair.

A paltry film of sweat rests on
her forehead, flashing like dew
in the disappearing light.
Her breasts, sweet and pure
of perfect shape and size,
suitable for any sculptor's critical eye.

Slow cadence, rhythmical movement
like Aphrodite was her teacher, God!
She must have been the prize pupil,
even her walk is a catchy melody.
Her arms cross about her smooth
delightful belly adding new meaning
to the word enticing.

She is a gateway to a new world,
my personal escape to take delight
in ecstasy.
My heart swells with pride
as I realize that this splendid goddess
affirms my faith that God is love
and she his ultimate creation.

Portrait

Your face is put together
of alien pieces
like some exploited view
of a mystic puzzle.
Above a defiant nose,
made lewd and pornographic
by its broad, flat bridge
lie two searching eyes
refusing to define their color.
Your lips, even closed,
dance and sing for me,
inviting me to come
so close
that you redden like your cheeks
in sudden rage at the risk
of discovery, defying exploration
like some desolate island
destined to be conquered.

Steamy Windows

Whether they know it or not, they
are secure only in their embrace.
Yet they sit here, back seat instruction
by nervous apprentices compensating
expertise with such vigilant diligence.
Her blouse has gathered slowly upward folds,
sweater creased, hair broken free
from the order of the barrette.
He sits uncomfortable, glasses as if alien
to his face, shirt bound tightly
to the body's rigid expectations.
Their security does not lie in cramped
legs sprawled sideways or horizontal
motion, but only in their embrace.

Masking Faces

She's at her dressing table while
I sit by, hushed, unmoving,
a spectator in this ritual
as she peels free
those long furry lashes,
withdraws some terribly strategic
pin or clasp and lets her hair
fall freely upon her shoulders.
Removing color, tone, shading
from each and every hill
and hollow of her face.
She stands quietly in the half light
appraising herself,
adjusting the return of
that naked face people never see.
I swallow deeply,
reviewing the return of
that naked face,
trying not to let her see
how easy it is to trust myself
each time I witness
her nightly unmasking
and discover that
this woman is most beautiful
when she is most plain.

Words Hurt

We are not speaking of love
or anything resembling it,
only of mutual friends
and how we'll be under some guarded eye
to prevent anything like attraction turning to
something else that might surprise
and maybe capture us.

I can see in your eyes the fear
of finding out and know my heart
is never wrong except when I tell it otherwise.
We don't talk of love
or be alone to discuss it or us,
better to keep it bottled until ripe or spoiled
whatever the recipe for security in these matters.

We don't talk or speak or even mutter the word.
Better that we let it push
and pull and stretch and make
our innards scream than to let it show.
Often I think about your advice
and how it is all too correct
but it doesn't help when all I can do is listen.

It's a Matter of Time

I say you're beautiful,
you say "average".
I compliment your smile
and you just shrug.
Later I said I want you
and you laughed, saying "why"?
Why?
Why not let down your guard
just long enough
to be what I want you to be?
It won't hurt, I promise.
You'll still be the same in the mirror
but I'll see more from this angle.
Why do I feel that I'm fleecing emotions
to make this work?
I'll only take advantage to make us closer
and to keep Father Time at bay.
You turn away,
no smile or smirk
and I know you
are Cinderella and that it's too late,
past midnight for us
but I'm still trying to hold the hour arm
long enough to enjoy your company
before the minutes pose us harm.

Split Personality

Some of them wanted the dancer
for the glistening sweat shining in the summer eve
or simply because it reminded them of one they lost.
Some said they wanted the writer
so they could see the words they so
wanted to hear but only read.
Some yet still wanted the boxer
with the body contoured to fit the regimen
of sculptured fantasy when the lights were dimmed.
Some just wanted the white shirt and suit
because the W-2 can be as comforting as any arms
and it solved their problem, after all.
Still I wait for the one that wants me for me,
the most important one who waits to see what
tomorrow will bring.

A Tribute to Rap Music

Yo.

Short Introduction

alone in a grove of silent eyes
the gasping amps flicker sounds
vibrantly across a large room
and last night I was one not unlike
any other waiting an unknown lover

. . . and later I saw her again
wearing loveliness as a shield, I
wearing loneliness as a weapon
black haired, dark eyed sweetsour
twenty-one o God what pleasure, what
happiness might, could, would have been. . .

if maybe I'd come but only
a few years earlier to this exact
spot, table, scent of beer
and stood alone and smiled
and she and I and waiting lives
in this noisy dive
that now brings back memories
of empty dreams and lost desires.

First Lover (Anne)

The immense monuments
Erected by man's ego,
Will lie in dust
On the floor of infinity
Before I lose your memory.

Wasteful wars burn in doom,
The poet's powerful rhyme
Forgotten in time
While your eyes
Dwell in my memory.

The passing of posterity
Weeps, for it cannot
Wipe your living memory.

To you who made the lover sigh
And gave what money could not buy.

I'm the Dancer (Chris)

A dancer in darkness pleading for your hand
so some day we can show
we've led a life of our own.
Our lives are other men's means,
so fall emperors and queens.
Nations arise and nations fall
changing not people but only names
in the end all remains the same.
They serve to kindle other fires
with rancid remnants of their own desires.
There is no single song
soothing its listeners for long
except escape with me.

Romantic

Ecstasy not happiness,
tragedy, not just failure.
A bonfire, not just a flame,
"Who's Who" obviously
a byline wouldn't do.
So if I ask you
if you're the answer to my dreams
or just another nightmare
remember that you're dealing
with one dabbling in extremes.
The difference between good
and great is measured in millimeters not miles
so I try to maintain the pace,
nobody remembers who finished in second place.

What You Want To Hear

Come visit me soon,
pretty child,
and bring your
gifts of youth
when you come.
I will give you
wine with your dinner,
love on the linoleum,
a flower on Thursdays,
dancing every Saturday.
I'll shave before passion,
my coat when its cold,
and a poem
etched with your eyebrow pencil
on the bathroom mirror
each morn of our life
so youth will never leave you,
nor love betray me.

I Dance Too

Wet open mouths,
hosts to rigid tongues
in their silent duel.
A contest for the passionate,
each tongue performs with practiced skill
the expected maneuvers.
There are rules to the game;
intensity is painted with
always predictable gestures
on skin that pretends to respond.
We collide and join.
My body goes with yours,
a part of me
staying behind to watch the performance
as a jaded critic
of my grotesque ballet.

Dawn

and two lovers
rise up out
of the slumbers
of night with
their dreams of
each other and
of nameless things that
remain a passionate
mystery strolling
the paths of
prior nights, and
they dream the day away together
or apart, to dream of their next
meeting, meaning, or mostly of the other's name.

Practices and Partners

"A good relationship is a 50/50 proposition."

Oh sage, what wisdom you have,
how right you are for the wrong reason.
Everything is a partner of sorts,
Messrs. Saks and Macy knew of that
long ago in different form.
Today I blew in your ear,
(another of my silly gestures)
and you gave back a sly smile.
For a squeeze of your hand
you offer a gentle kiss,
for a fluttering of my eyelids
you grant a silly laugh,
and for my tears sometimes
late in the night you make
your breast a soothing pillow
and with your hands a comforting shield
against the fears for which I have no name.
We practice this lost art together,
a game of give and take—but
each of us have no greed for profit,
only the need to be an honest trader.

Gravity (Does Not Change Your Mind)

If only I believe what I'm seeing,
the rounded shoulders and jello breasts
fortified on those dwarfed thick legs.
Thank God for my clever wit not to say anything at first
and for the mind's eye
that keeps recollections dimmed
most conveniently at times like this!

How cruel to cremate old visions
when beauty skin deep
(or was it deep folds of skin) are recollected on
mornings like cheap films that came as often as the
sun didn't meet us at dawn,
but we didn't have the energy to care.
How reluctant I am to dust your memory.
The thought of your marriage brushed aside,
chauvinistically you'll always be mine,
first possession being nine-tenths of the law.
It is sometimes hard getting blisters again
from the impersonal burns of the past
but I keep you imprisoned yet in our tainted childhood,
I have only pretended to grow older.
Only our skills and groping have become educated
and acceptable, but our bodies
have continued to age.

Intro To Life 101

Introductions in bars
he is a professor of knowing people,
erudite of faces in a room, though there is no chair
on the subject at the university.
In the night working on his papers,
educated fingers finger his papers
as he would finger a thigh.
But his head is a bookcase of oft quoted volumes,
classic words excite his mouth.
Odd that some 19 naive big eyed girl can
make the scholar's skin break into glistening
hot scented sweat, destroying a thousand years
of civilized cultivation farmed into his head.
Such is the introduction of young teachers to Life 101.

Virgin

After that
breathless instant
of shattering,
throbbing, piercing
and yielding
penetration
deep within,
and everything
lying suddenly
still, the immersion
with all life;
wonder, shock
and the gentle ticking
of the hallway clock;
tearing, ripping and
heavy breathing—a
human experience is now complete.

After the Thrill is Gone

Same dances in the same old shoes
some habits that you just can't lose
there's no telling what a man might do
after the thrill is gone.
The flame rises but it soon descends
empty pages and a frozen pen
you're not quite lovers and you're not quite friends
after the thrill is gone.

What can you do when your dreams come true
and it's not quite like you planned?
What have you done to be losing the one
you held it so tight in your hand.
Time passes and you must move on
half the distance takes you twice as long
so you keep on singing for the sake of the song
after the thrill is gone.

You're afraid you might fall out of fashion
and you're feeling cold and small
any kind of love without passion
ain't no kind of loving at all.
Same dances in the same old shoes
you get too careful about the steps you choose
you don't care about winning
but you don't want to lose
after the thrill is gone.

AFTER THE THRILL IS GONE — **Copyright, Benchmark Music and Kicking Bear Music. Written by Glenn Frey and Don Henley. Performed on the album ONE OF THESE NIGHTS by The Eagles on Asylum Records. Special thanks to Glenn and Don for their kind permission to use this song in the book. Also, thanks for the inspiration, your other works and support.**

Paupers and Profiteers

Six of a dozen, half of the other.
A prince, a pauper, a lover and a thief.
One to trust and the other to steal,
it's getting harder to know who to believe.
When you're not taken, you're being took,
see him in the mirror, see him on the street
searching for another adventure, anything chic,
lurking to steal all within reach.
Profiteer interest in money foretold
pauper's destiny is but fool's gold.
White hat villains and black hat Samaritans,
all accounted for on the balance sheet.
Designer suits or plain tee shirts,
one has a hand in your pocket
while the other's got his hand in your soul.
You think you're safe from others
when suddenly it appears
you've become your own victim,
the prey of your own fear.
Paupers and profiteers, all in their own splendor,
nothing gained except in surrender,
from yourself to yourself, from pauper to profiteer.

Torch Song

The smell is in the air again.
That summer smell after the rain
robs the evening of humidity.
I remember that smell too well,
that weekend in Indiana with
the harsh words spoken to mock whatever moot point
we were bitterly contesting.

That smell is in the air again.
The last time the air was this heavy
you licked the beads of perspiration off the A & W mug,
threw back your head
and I watched your earrings dance.
To this day each time
the heat shimmers off the summer road
your image dances before me.
You wore your pout then like a proud inheritance
and I was glad you called the bout long enough to
let the show unfold before me.
The ritual was a dance performed without audience,
we became one during the presentation.

That smell is in the air again and I remember how I
never forgave myself for saying goodbye
because I wanted to be part of the encore.
But it happened too quickly like the dew
awakening your feet
 then disappearing in the August sun.
I wanted to be a part of the act and the encore
and often sorry I didn't sign up
for a lifetime performance.

Nothing's Changed

That split second sentiment,
your impulsive passion and cool detachment,
dancing yourself to sweat.
And I took you later to again speed your pulse
making a scavenger hunt of erotic pleasures.
After, you say that you are done playing
musical beds but the tune will begin again
and the only change will be us making love together
with another face.
But I've been bored at parties
and overheard your name
dropped by a casual informant
and my heart unfurled
like a morning flower unprotected,
past events wrestled current thoughts and
I had no choice but to recall your eyes.
It is then that I realize the weight of regret,
once again your soft voice and softer smile
brighten the night.
For a brief minute I rejoice
wishing the events were so arranged
that recollection bears no pain—yet it does,
and in the end
I find that nothing's really changed,
and that tomorrow (at the very latest)
each of us will again be making love
together to another face.

Exorcism

Somebody mentioned your name today
and that ghost rose from wherever it was resting,
flooding my head with memories, the kind that
hurt yet you learn to live with.
It wasn't hard to remember
how we learned about love
from each other, groping in back seats,
back yards and mostly with ourselves.
It wasn't hard to remember
how your smile could scare away
the morning fog in autumn
or make a summer day seem like it
would never end.

Still, in the back of my head I know how the look in your
eye could calm the blowing rain (or so it seemed).
Then we were sixteen/twenty
and nothing was ever going to change.
So still not totally believing the change
I wrestle that ghost—
not wanting to win, for if I did, the haunting
would end and I still feel some warm through the ashes
though the flame has expired.
There will be no exorcism of the past,
no rite of passage for the haunting.
For the loss of memory is more painful
than the hurt of remembering.

Notes To Myself

Please remember that
one day she will slip
away from under these covers
and a new set of fingers
will trace lines across
her face, a new body will
tan in her affection.
No. Yes—don't play divine
right to her (thank God for
the constant companion of
diplomacy, the conscience).

It is certain enough, like
the rising and falling of
sexual folly and the seldom
seen sun in a Toledo winter.
But please remember when you
leave, close the door
lightly, ever gently, and
always know there is no lock.

There is no constant champion.
My time is due, my fallen hair
is witness enough.
Remember this summer breeze
and the words I should have said
but instead kept in notes like this
to remain unsaid.
But please remember the door
is never locked, even if some
words were carefully guarded.

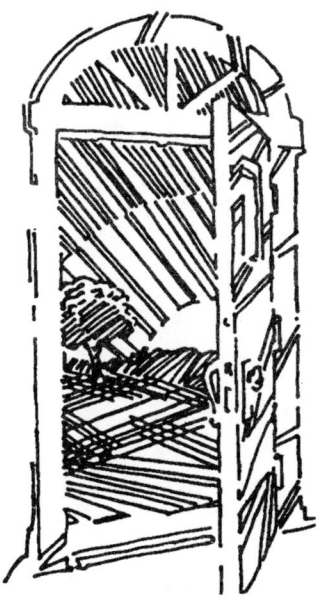

The Walk

It was your walk.
God, what a walk!
Your legs fell out of
the bottom of your short coat
and your feet never landed
the same twice.
Infinite movements,
you were someone new
each time you took a step.

You rescued my day
pretty young girl.
A thousand like you
have decorated a thousand days for me.
The city overflows with you.
I used to want to meet you,
confirm my fantasies,
discover your secrets,
explore your delights.
Not any more.
I'm older now.
I need the mystery.

Passing Years

There is no certain fate for the
kind that seeks out the naked beauty
or beast camouflaged
behind the costumed mask.
Their fate I understand, their
images easy to spot—wearing love
on blue jeans or on car bumpers.
I have loved them behind doors and
all night bars, remember their arms
and smiles and the delicate way they
defend themselves from themselves.
A noble attempt for such foolish reasons.
My fate is stored in some Grimm's tale,
their mock heroics easier to understand.
I grow soft in my aging but
they have grown a bit harder through
the passing years, like candy that sits
on shelves and their interiors no longer
melt in your mouth.
One night I heard one of them say she wished to
love someone young again.
At the same time another said she wished
I were younger for the same reason—hoping
for taut muscles to again envelope her
and take her mind off herself.
Victims of confused maturity,
lost without a map, not knowing enough to look
to the stars to see where they are.
I know their meaning and their wants,
but nothing of their pain, so I nod to them
in silent agreement, knowing that to seek
out the player from the program you must
be aware of passing years and the pleasant
fears with which they are a part.
There is no certain fate for these women
who are not strangers to love
but know hurt as a constant companion,
and never have the magic potion
to find their champion.

Carpe Diem

Stop listening to the voices
of your creators
denying your existence.
They have nothing to do with you now,
and all the prohibitions
were only the anguished
screams of their mortality.
So enter yourself
when I do,
and listen only to
the laughter of your skin
while we treat ourselves
to forbidden lusts
and secret places.
If the only point worth proving
is pleasure,
then be your most selfish self
for pleasing you pleases me.
After all, the bed is the only place
where we give only with the expectation of receiving.
So trust me
when I tell you we'll be
getting our money's worth.
Ignore me when I play
because you have taught
my tongue how to dance,
and a thousand nights from now
I will close my eyes
to let my body remember
the joyous taste of you.

Surrender

From a thousand
Sealy mattresses have
I climbed—or more it seems.
None seemed more satisfied
at the time, their
applause drew my bow.

A hundred luscious maidens
have shared their prurient dreams
or more—it seems.
They found me too much
in command to offer
the intimacy eluding them.

You need no evidence
of my trust.
No witnesses
to witness
on your behalf.
"Methinks the lad hath protested
too, too many times
in the past and present."
And now I only want to hear
from you during and after private moments.

Phone Calls

I leave a note
on every Camaro in
the parking lot with
a message;

    Is anything wrong?
        I'm sorry.
        I miss you!
        Please call.
        474-2140

I receive many calls,
inquiries to my height
and the color of my eyes, but
most simply reply
"I miss you and it's
lonely here too."

Graceful Deceit

I lied you know,
by not telling you before
that love meant more than being warm
on days when snow clings to the window.
I lied, very well I think
by holding back information,
that getting up at six for work
and arguing over TV shows to watch
takes the edge off sleeping together late.
I broke some kind of commandment
but feel no wrong.
I could have said that love is
getting what you need when you want
and just hoping for the rest.
I lied, but for the sake of semantics call it a fib,
for love is giving, giving not for love
but for getting back your desires
and putting up with poetic liars.

First Impressions

The way you walked in the room
made me pledge my lust to you.
You looked like a party favor
waiting to be unwrapped.
In haste I remembered that dare I reach too far
I'd lose the smile and even the innocent touch
and be looking like everyone else from behind
the glass wishing for more
of something that I could never have.
The way you smiled when you turned around
made you a magnet to the heads in the room
and I tried, really I did, to turn away.
I thought about trying to kill your smile
before another could pilfer it
but it really doesn't bother me
when I see the looks looking except
those times when I see you glancing back.

The Misinformed, Losers and the Heartbroken

The misinformed, losers and the heartbroken,
together in this place, a seedy carnival attraction
parking in half lit booths and
watching,
watching,
always watching and waiting, playing this odd scene.

The misinformed, losers and the heartbroken
jaywalking through conversations, topical nonsense
and buzzwords of "would you know",
"how about it" and "look at her".
Esoteric nonsense leaping from their mouths
dying midst the din of the crowd
these believers in tarots,
capricorns and moons ascending.
Who will have the heart to tell these mannequins
dangling in sharkskin, silver and gold?
Who would have the heart to tell them
that age and youth have different truths
and they who doubt nothing know nothing?

The misinformed, the losers, oh, the losers.
Always too old to set a bad example,
always to quick to give advice.
From their kindness jumps vulgarity,
cruelty flies from their insincerity.
Nothing is as boring as conversation with the righteous
"has beens, never were's
and won't happen no how's",
secure in the wisdom of their ignorance,
truly worthy apostles.

The misinformed, losers and the heartbroken—
the heartbroken know their destiny.
K-Tel sells their love songs,
their charisma worn like faded linoleum.
Theirs is the security that life is as fertile as neurosis.
Pass another round of sympathy
for they are long dead,
refusing to climb in the box and to shut the lid.
It is part of the education, training in residence,
but there will be no applause for theirs is a moaning
venereal disease and nothing to clap about.

Lost Kiss

We have rediscovered innocence
you and I.
Our love is no longer
a sure thing.
There are no guarantees
between us.
No inevitabilities to blur the present.
Kissing is a stolen piece of pie,
jealously guarded,
devoured with greedy ritual,
the feast of Bacchus.
The touching of our lips
could someday be enough
to occupy a thousand lifetimes
but it is only the beginning,
the first heartbeat
of our one day learning the art of nuance,
able to please each other
across crowded rooms.

Tables Turned

What's on your mind tonight?
Why do you click the light
laughing like you do?
Gentlemen are a dying race,
this isn't right,
click it on again!
It's not because of the way you walk
drifting down the street,
it's not apparent in the way you talk
doing things with your feet,
or the way you sway your hair
that makes the odor sweet.
A fellow's not made of glass
and poets not made of steel.
Some of the time this guy's an ass
some of the time a heel,
some of the time a shot down god,
and that's the way I feel.
Love the American Way you deserve
but not from this old boy to serve—
there's more than a kiss on the lips
a grip on the . . . breast
and sudden dive into the pelvis.

Wholesale

Seldom now does the present
catch the past.
It's a game of chance,
yesterday playing tag
but not swift enough to touch it.
I regret sometimes for-once-
known-love because more time
is spent remembering than seeking
new directions and capturing
that "once-upon-a-time" thing again.
But a poor man rejoices in worlds
where things are free,
everyone equally rich,
although sometimes I equally regret
that a few were mighty cheap.

Postage Due

I threw away the letters
you had sent me, perhaps
in anger, perhaps in play.
But I don't want you staying
now that I've found whatever it was
we stayed up all night
trying to find with words that lost
their way from my side
of the room to yours.
They are all ashes now, your misspellings
and habits not punctuated by discovery.
I even burned my finger
to rid me completely of any second thoughts.
I threw away your letters because
I refuse to play moth to your burning desires,
because the letters were sent in play
and I was reading them in anger.

Doors Have Knobs On Both Sides

You are always on the outside
gawking like a child through a window,
nose pressed tightly over the candy display.
    You want but are afraid.
        you want but take no risk.
        You want but will not give.
        You want but will . . . what?
                what fanciful excuse
have you for today, yesterday and tomorrow?
Expend, give to receive.
Even the smallest creature in nature lives for
its own gain, even the fiercest have need.
Not even the flowers wild in the forest
are self-sustaining.
Have you broken the
universal order of life?
Growing up is more than having money
and a four door that gets you around.
You are afraid that once the door is opened
perhaps it will leave you trapped,
you don't know or care to know that doors open
      or close
on both sides
like fences that close
both in or out at the same time.
    I cannot bring my world to you,
        it is too full of swinging doors and fences
        that are constantly in use.
It would be better to be a stairway in life
that at least has a starting and ending point
than to be an escalator moving, always moving
and yet never leading anywhere but back to its origin.
    I cannot bring my world into yours,
for you offer to spend no part of yourself
and wait for another to first try the door.
The invitation is there, but gambling means
losing more if you have wagered nothing.

Is The Pope Catholic?

"Hello sweet thing . . .
Do I remember you?
I remember you like a porcupine
is remembered for its quills.
I remember you like a tree remembers
the surgeon that severs its limb.
Luckily they regenerate,
I only grew tissue over the dream you
sliced with your razor ways.
I remember you on early March mornings
when the air suddenly turns white
flying dead from my mouth.
I suppose I remember you best when
I see men hammering oak
stakes into mother nature like
a vampire that won't die.
I remember you all too well,
but every time you fade I recall
how a man was stitched head to toe after a
crash and wonder what medicine has
will bandage a bloodied heart.
I remember, yes, I remember you as a splinter
too deep to cut loose, like a hangman
is known by his noose.

Words And Music By . . . (to Greg)

Give me a pen and some ink,
give me a quiet place to think.
Let me have some place in this busy life,
free from trouble, scorn and strife,
to gather my thoughts and give them voice
by writing them down in words of choice.
A word, a phrase, something sage—
someday to be discovered
or from an attic drawer uncovered.
But until then, I write on and on and on,
proud words on a dusty shelf.
Too damn bad that they'll be found
so long after I'm dead and gone.

Birthday Girl

She stands in front of her mirror in somewhat
a puzzled way, for today the girl has grown up,
today the girl has her birthday.
She remembers times when she wore party hats
and blew whistles, her father's gentle tease,
brother grabbing at the presents, aunts sending
her things she didn't need.
She notices the blondish curls have given way
and she thinks of her parents at rest, the
older brother who lost his life
and little sister — god knows what she's done.
She stares in front of the mirror in a sad
and gloomy way, today's the day to celebrate
but her day is far from gay.
This time, time has taken the fun and whistles
and left her the remains.
She bends to inspect the lines by her eyes,
blaming gravity for her decay.
Standing like a stranger searching the mirror out,
not sure anymore how she's to look.
Today's the day for her birthday
so she pushes her book aside,
reads the cards sent to the 60-year-old girl
who celebrates her birthday by herself.

Between The Lines

There's never much to say between
the moments of our games and repartée
There's never much to read between
the lines of what we need
and what we'll take
There's never much to talk about
or say aloud, but say it anyway
Of holidays, and yesterdays,
and broken dreams that somehow slipped away

In books and magazines of how to be
and what to see while you are being
Before and after photographs teach
how to pass from reaching to believing
We live beyond our means
on other people's dreams
and that's succeeding
Between the lines of photographs
I've seen the past — it isn't pleasing

> so strike another match
> We'll have another cup of wine
> and dance until the evening's dead
> of too much song and time
> There's never much to speak about
> or read between the lines of what we
> dream about when we're apart
> and no one's looking on to say
> "You're mine"

It was a good year then
It was a good year then — we all remember
the time you threw the looking glass
and seemed a fool — or very clever
Don't spoil it all; I can't recall
a time when you were struck
without an answer
We'll live a quiet, peaceful time
between the lines, and go together

We'll dance until we've
killed another evening off
Don't think of anyone but me
I'll have no lovers on the side
Tonight is all we've ever dreamed about
For once, let's get it right
I'll go down flying in the end
Throw another bottle in between the lines
I'll go down like a ship of state
so let's be gracious now
between the lines

BETWEEN THE LINES — Copyright, Mine Music LTD/April Music, Inc. Written and performed by Janis Ian on the album BETWEEN THE LINES, CBS Records. Thanks, Janis, for "Between the Lines, Stars & Aftertones" and your kind help.

Sports Heroes and Cheerios

It is funny.
It smacks of mirth.
To see the young bulls pacing
sidelines in hope of entering the game
for the winning touchdown or bucket
so they'll have something to remember
twenty years hence.
It is funny, you know?
To see them training for the sport,
to be for one fleeting moment
the dancer on the field stage.
Their movements seem fluid enough
and the best of them actually have grace.
I always sit behind the cheerleaders who greatly
contribute to the victory but never defeat,
always with a smirk or foolish grin on my face
wondering about the dignity
of satin panties and cartwheels.
In the aftermath the jocks will probably
realize nursing their Buds and carefully
making their appointed weights that either way
they lose, a realization somewhat too late.
To see that love makes, anger and passion
fake, the sake of the lesson they are trying
to seek.
It is funny from where I sit
to know that sports create the exercise
but the dancer creates art.
Ah, the view I have from here.
Can I reach a conclusion from this valuable
experience and from such diligent thought?
Ah, yes! Sport is for the hoofers not able
to pass the artistic test.

In The Stretch

You've still the same pretty face
but a wrinkle or two's been introduced.
Still have the golden throat
but your catchy tunes are aging.
Tell me star what you're going to do
when the glitter loses its sparkle,
and the dream floats down like a balloon
two days after the county fair?
You still possess that handsome figure
but the belt is one notch longer.
Always beating the odds, oh yes,
but a worthy opponent is the clock.
Your naughty lines still make people squirm,
what happens when they've heard them all?
Can you still cut it in the dance halls?
Hair still falls in place, but those extra bows
catch a glimpse of your spotty crown.
Will you write a touching tune to overcome
or stumble from the charts?
Think about selling the shiny Mark IV
and check into the Ford,
when the records don't sell
it's back to the old man's store.
The guitar has seen better days,
better keep running to set the pace
nobody pays to see second place.

A Tribute To Rod McKuen
(and various outlandish places)

if i see you in Peking,
on some steps in Amsterdam
or strolling naked on an Albanian beach
i will try to break the news gently
that happiness is eating pizza while going
through a car wash in Topeka
and if we meet under unusual circumstance
i will tell you the agony of life—
having nine cents when you need a
pay toilet in the streets of Helena
and other romantic places.

should we meet at McDonalds in Bulgaria
i will give you words meaningful in quest saying things
only poets share;
that the secret of life is on matchbook covers
or in the manholes of Milwaukee
freedom a journey on a Concord jet bound for Uganda
reached only by those who have nothing
to begin with and less to lose.
keep writing old man, keep trying,
for Utopia is always on the other side of the street
gurus and yogurt help ease the pain—
but love is varicose veins in villas
in Paris or Venice.

Gift

What I gave you
You cannot take from me forcefully
In the darkness between us.
In this way I win twice—I gain
The joy of giving,
And leave you nothing to steal.

Genealogy

"THE CHILD IS THE FATHER TO THE MAN"
Wm. Wordsworth

Thanks Larry, Moe and Curly Joe
for the rap on the head that made me laugh,
for showing me funny for funny's sake as a way of life—
more than merely something
during a commercial break.
Thanks for the ability to look at myself and see
the humor in the things of which I have no grace,
for knowing the expressions and rude noises
that bring smiles to many an otherwise sad face.
Thanks Messrs. Astaire, Kelly and Cary Grant
for the song and dances, for being debonair,
making me aware of ordinary treasures
that told me life and love are ordinary small pleasures.
Thanks Abbott, Costello and Andy Clyde,
Jack Benny, Buster Keaton, Spanky and the Gang,
for bringing me up on twenty-year-old flicks
that made me boo and hiss and cheer,
put me to bed with skits and antics
dancing in my head.
Thanks for the tales that never preached
but always managed to teach wrong from right.
Thanks again one and all.
For those who sang and danced,
taught me why I cry and laugh,
I know your time has passed
but forever you've achieved posterity
and seek a place and part
of history and immortality.

Two Trees Only Grow Next To Another Never One Under The Other

Gaining audience is no difficult task.
It requires only a moment of babble,
some age old small talk about the weather
as if we truly were concerned.
But now we are together for some time
and again we become nervous strangers
as if we met again after a separation
and feared the quality of our talk.
We must renew our acquaintance
and again take pleasure in our varied
past and the uncertain path of our words.
Too long I've spent trying to please,
too long I've spent trying to remain me
instead of taking chances on change.
Should I risk stopping knowing that
when something green stays the same
that its remains are a heap of brown debris?
How can we be right for each other,
if we are at best bookends
stationed on a dusty shelf?
This painful process must begin again,
manners put aside.
Let us grow and face it together
like two trees sharing life,
live together like two trees
given nature's distance,
neither overshadowing the other.

Road Pizza

Bone and blood and fur
thrown to the side
and sometimes in the middle of the road.
Driving by at 65 m.p.h. the breeze always rustles
the fur and it remains for days
lying on its side untouched.
How is it that their faces are never seen?
Were they all hit at that last minute
without seeing the end?
And do you think that the thunk of the tires
at all disturbs their slumber?
Do the crews that pry the remains
from this skillet road ever
wonder why they committed suicide this way?

Magic

I have tricks in my pockets
And, yes, things up my sleeve.
No, I'm not a stage magician,
He gives an illusion
Which has the appearance of truth.
I offer the truth
In a pleasant disguise of illusion.

The Home

Her hands are heavily veined and wrinkled,
Her mind filled with memories untold.
Nobody cares to listen to her
Simply because she is old.

The young ones come out of duty
And stay a very short while.
They discuss weather, other nonsense
And sit with a nervous smile.

The older ones come and patronize
And correct the things she has done.
They seem to forget so easily
That the old still like to have fun.

To think someday that I'll be old,
Will these sometime visitors yet arrive?
They'll not recall a body limber, only old.
The body battered, tired but forgetting
That the mind's very much alive.

Cheerleader

The men of Central High,
padded, garbed for their weekly fight
trod unto the field under neon light,
a fearful sight of designed might.

The nipping biting wind
gives ample cause for Holiday cheer
to be passed around and chants dance in the air
from ear to ear.

The sidelines this night arrest my eye,
gazing at your skirt so slight,
fluttering in the December breeze
forcing me to sigh.

Staring at your school sweater
draped from your slender shoulders,
showcasing the blossoming of young womanhood
the school insignia.

Chafed lips
quivering at each blast the wind provides,
munching your exposure.
Bobbing frantically, urging the men to supremacy
your red glowing knees
shine like Uncle Henry's cheeks
last Christmas Eve.

Your presence insinuates
a statue, a goddess
studied last in classics class.

Glancing about, all my neighbors
chanting cheers with deaf mouths
and the releasing of rehearsed motions.
Turning, blinded by the towers illuminating the stadium
I realized that you are as artificial as the sacrifice
in the false day,
like the bulbs lighting the night in the wrong way.

Slaughterhouse (Why I'm a Vegetarian)

The slaughterhouse violence has ceased
for the day, only the
socketless exposed eye
disturbs the night guard dozing
in the somnolent reek.

The fragrance of meatdust
sprayed generously from band saws
scents the floor with layers of fat
sawed organs, splashed dark blood,
the tiny purple rivulets flowing
into vast vats in thick streams.

The bulks of flesh
wrapped in spotted gauze and brown paper
dangling in swaying motion
from death hooks reminds the housewife
of the event-filled massacre.

The crashing axe fracturing skull,
scattering fragments of listless bone from
within the once taunt skin enclosure,
and heads sprawled carelessly over a barrel,
sawdust absorbing drained life.

The pin sticking in throat's tip,
probing jugular scream,
agonizing death this
carcass butchering.

The aroma of rawness,
trademark of sadistic enterprise
$4.99 "For this?" the shopper complains
while unions bargain for a living wage,
nobody wondering who is sane.

Love's Labor (Grandma Tess)

"A heart is not judged by how much you love,
but by how much you are loved by others."
      The Wizard of Oz to the Tin Man

A young girl's dream and her man's eager fancy
leaping childhood memories to career and family.
Fairy tale transition into reality,
the cocoon spun to hard times.
Money never held much promise,
the table had to be set with meat,
and dresses and movies took a back seat,
always indefinitely postponed.
Little mouths keep regular meals
even when the income didn't keep pace.
Time always ran behind it seemed
so never was it really much of a race.
So changed vacations,
pleasures and weekend schemes,
and worries, oh worries—a constant challenge
to patience and personal dreams.
Thick and thin, lean and pork-barrel years
hope stretched its head so high,
and optimism—thank God it never showed
even to the least bit shy.
Bedrooms slowly emptied
and children went their way,
laundry dwindled and the icebox got a break,
but the hair kept turning gray.
The children begot their children all too soon
and pocket money reappeared.

Soon the end begins again,
the fourth generation starts another wave.
Two in the beginning again reunite,
the young girl's dream now history,
her man awaiting her sight.
For the first time never had the leisure
even for a goodbye, but now they'll find the time
again to dream of each other
and toast their lips to wine,
together again as beginning to end
the roots of the family vine.

Time

I spent the evening listening
to her roller coaster memory running
round and round and up and down,
and turned and turned over decades
of history that took hours and hours
when teachers recited in school.
Strange how time floats from life to life
traversing generations instantly, a blink of the eye.
Listening to the events described in ritual fashion,
I see the signs so subtle, like the boy
who goes to shave and instead sees his father's face.
Change makes cowards of us all
and she talks from faulty memory
while meandering like an old river
with a voice not dimmed by age
yet forgets her son's name.
Sometimes she sets the table for two
even though it's been five odd years since
he passed away, almost to the day.
I just smile when she calls me by another name,
nodding in agreement as her glazed stare waves
past me into the past or future relived
or regretted one more time.
When she catches her own look she will be disturbed,
so politely I'll look away again and say nothing when
again called by another name
during a midsentence nap.
By morning she will forget, instead remember another
face and time stretching
the edges of her mind, practicing
the art of living today and remembering yesterday.
There are layers of inherited tissue protecting
the scars she has learned to use to survive.
I leave without a word while the ticking clock in the
hallways chants its refrain praying that it will
not be wound too many more mornings.
"Tis the last rose of summer" . . . said Keats, and she is.

Conception

Seed of life nurtured
in mother's fertile womb
about to be butchered,
buried without tomb;
I address you.

How shall the epitaph read
etched above your head
while you're safely smothered dead
in a plastic disposable bed?

The thought far removed that night
was anything but creating life.
So you innocent infant will bear the knife
and endure the strife
scraped to ease mother's plight.

Shining silver sides severs
life's cord, dispensing with teeming life.
How will all this rest
when all is said
and answering at best that mother wasn't a wife?

And when suddenly appears
those legally sterilized shears,
plowing life's canal,
unsuspecting you'll leer.

Your frail fetus stage
with courts ruling God's might
bellowing individual rights,
will you be given to testify
out of your own invite?

For every human regardless of age
forgiving love's entangled snare
flushing life at a rapid pace,
then bowing gently saving grace
leaving blood money in the plate,
is seeking forgiveness for their race.

Oh, mother if you only ponder
ourselves as carriers of life,
incipient grows to separateness
and its own meaning.
Life, is and is not,
there is no nothingness.

Today

Today I live
Each minute
Without fear,
For beneath
The surface
Of tomorrow
Lie the many
Promises that
Didn't exist
Yesterday.

Sounds of Love

The sounds of love are harsh
to the ear,
the breaking dish,
whimper in the dark
when the lights are turned out
and the embarrasing red around the eye.
The harshest of the sounds
are those of the last word barely spoken—
goodbye.

Higher Education

I learned about pain
when my left crossed his jaw
and two teeth, assorted gum and
blood sprinted to the ground.
Hurt I learned at seventeen
and turned away the girl
I loved for false bravado.
Thrill was the genuine smile
from the child who knows nothing of
sixteen hours at the office.
I discovered the power of the written word
when you read my page and cried.
But I learned about love today from the
old couple at the zoo.
He patted the old girl
on the ass, threw back his head
and roared with laughter.
I've learned that blue hair
can spark mischievous behavior.

Old What's Her Name

I've read you in a thousand books,
heard your name in a thousand songs.
You're more than respected in the plays I've seen
and poets can't capture enough of you
to keep their rhymes and verse clean.

I've heard the sages speak of you,
and know you're the magic in the act
of renowned legerdemain.
You are like the dew in the morning
that nobody knows where it goes,
the rainbow after the storm that
artists sketch in awe.

The names are all the same, though they
be rearranged, and never once did any
of them catch you for more than a second
before you disappeared.
You're the muse of art and the demon of death,
the creation of the wicked mind.
You are the reason that men live
and the choice of their death.

The Contribution of Disco Music

Second Wind

I feel like a kid again
discovering a new Mattel creation.
Sometimes these words spill from my head
without effort and God knows how long
it's been for that to be natural again.
My life was littered with regrets, that sort
of thing and I believed a great deal of what
I was told — that things were nice — things were good
and everything
was according to plan — that sort of thing.
But it wasn't and neither was I.
Trapped in some sort of cheap novel,
Mother Goose gone mad,
a Humpty Dumpty nightmare,
where there was not character, much less plot.
I endured like a mute without a clue as to
what the rest of the world spoke.
Years and years this went on like wearing a pair
of longies from head to toe that just made you itch
but you were more afraid to take them off because
of the cold . . . but I knew the cold most of all
and now seek out a warmer climate.
I did do the right thing, though for the wrong reasons.
I remember well what I had
but not too well why it's gone
and now forgotten like escalator stairs
always turning, turning, no beginning or end.
The turf remains the same but the grass
isn't any greener — I was.

Court and Spark

Already I've stumbled
and you've stubbed your toe as well.
We've got a lot in common
learning things all over again
like sleeping alone, chasing away old ghosts
that haunt you throughout some days
when you can't tell dark from light.
Perhaps a brief explanation,
refresher on the rules of the game . . . no.
We've got a lot in common,
already shared that fifth of therapy
and stuttered through conversation
littered with apology and regret.
But if your slender shoulders
can burden a few more fears
I'd like to walk into your eyes for a while
and what I see I promise not to tell.
We'll call a truce for the sake of emotional sabbatical.
We have a lot in common,
the weight of days that wouldn't end
when you felt so low that
even your shadow wouldn't show.
Willingly I'll offer my coat in winter
and my bed when you're cold
and shelter you from longing
until we're both tired and old.
Someday again we'll paintbrush the sky,
stop wondering about the past and why.
We've got a lot in common, you know?
Perhaps we still believe
after all the fairy tales we've been sold
and despite unanswered prayers,
that we've got a shot at the leprechaun's pot of gold.

Sundays Are For Suicide

Moments from now again I will be alone,
and I'm left with small fingerprints on the table
and assorted smudges
that mark my hours and time.
GI Joe and Ninja figures are lying
hopelessly in the din of battle
until the next "other weekend"
to again have their chance to save civilization.
Phantom footsteps hasten my look
into an empty hallway
but it is the reality of thirty-year-old buildings
to fool me in this not so pleasant manner.

I still awaken in the still of the night
sleepsearching for children who rest across town.
Sometimes I hear a cough and wonder if sound,
like pain, can be referred since they will not be
present until next Friday at the earliest.
While it can be annoying to hear their feet parade
in this space, it is far too lonely not to.
Returning to the fenced porch on Sunday
a silent scream erupts within
and the heart is again audible.
The tone again set once the door slams on my way out.
Forty eight hours are not enough when divided by four,
and if melancholy overtakes me
the obituary will state that
the cause of death
was the clock striking seven on Sunday.

Santa's Lap

The godlike position,
assumed in kingly splendor
is increased by the adoration
of innocent children who
nervously await their turn.

The tow headed boy
apprehensively approaches the throne
and sitting high upon the lap of this
man garbed in vestiged colors
gawks at the presence of snowbound whiskers
glued to his chin.

Lacking usual impishness
his manners are reserved and
prescribed by the situation.

One by one in singular fashion righteousness
is singularly proclaimed
and parents forget the chidings of the last fiscal year
as hope and promises lunge forward from speakers,
tinsled greetings in stereo.

Others wait in line rehearsing their plea,
some dressed in faded jeans and
flustered by their own boldness as they
proceed without parental hand
and stumble up the stairs to seek their due reward.
Others, afraid of discovery, dress in navy
jumpers and last year's suitcoats already too small
for the season.

The saint himself lures frail bodies with
peppermint sticks to those brave enough
to hear the wrath.
The sharp movements of those gaining audience is
the lesson of obedience, exposing themselves
and resolving never again to curse or disobey
daily commands of parents to love, honor and obey.

Occasionally a bulb flashes
blinding the god and child.
Parents smile broadly and snicker
knowingly so that some day when retired
they can again find glee
in these pictures and smug memories.

Waking the Dead

Why do you wake the dead?
Why probe the cadaver that
once was you and I?
It is over.
Finis.
Let it rest.
Do not dissect the whys, wherefore's
and heretofore's any longer.
The barristers have crossed the t's
and dotted even i.
Cast your scientific stare into the mirror
and reason and experiment as long as you desire.
There is no more fire,
no smouldering ash
to create any semblance of caring.
Let the corpse decay on its own terms,
I am not your forgiver nor pretender.
Let the dead rest.
Let them enjoy the slumber.
All the motions have been filed,
all the arguments have cut off any retreat,
left no room for compromise.
That cold steely glance and planning
have made public such a private thing.
So please leave the pulse of the wire alone
there is nothing more to say,
especially when you couldn't say it face to face
I certainly don't want to hear it on the phone.
So let it rest and both of us
will be able to spend a great deal of time,
side by side with nothing but our pride.

Nature's Way

Why the look of distress,
grimace as you glance in the mirror?
Lines a little more pronounced,
skin not nearly as taut.
There's more definition where it shouldn't be
and Snow White complexion no longer
like the inside of a tart apple,
though the taste be just as sweet.
Age is hell.
"Hush", you command breaking the soliloquy.
"Too much nonsense", you say.
No, what I see in my mind's eye is much clearer
than you wish to believe.
Glasses are taken off during love
for it is nature's way of compensating.
I need my glasses all the time except to remove them
when we love so that you still look the same to me.

Roll the Dice

The clouds are playing hide and seek
with the sun today,
like a shaman leaving some illusion on display
and my enthusiasm is left in the wake
of the daily ritual.
It puzzles me to know that
sometimes the simplest things
are the hardest to do,
the innocent hello,
the gentle nudge,
the little kiss,
and saying "it" forever
and meaning it for a long time.
If I appear cynical or the least bit skeptical
it's because over time I've seen
innocence kill the child in us
and know that spontaneity is best
when well thought out.
But I am ready to echo
over and over and over,
I will sing for you…
I will dance for you…
I will even play the fool for you…
In return I want promises –
soft smile in defeat,
to gloat in small victories.
Should doubt overwhelm me
as it sometimes wont to do,
a simple caress on the neck
for confidence till dawn.
Should sometimes I offend you
remember it's really in jest,
if sometimes my words fail you
or if they're just too true,
my pen will make amends
for when the heart speaks the soul listens.

So, if you don't play the quarry
I'll not be the hunter
and when it's said and done,
I'll swear each month we'll need new sheets
and never intentionally make you weep.
Come along for the ride
and stay by my side and keep my bed alive,
I promise never to live only from nine to five.
So I'm doing my best to figure
how to make a good first impression
the second time around.
In quest of the Golden Fleece
toast a toast to the American Dream
that we all receive our piece.
A nod, a wink, or simply a blink
and pretty soon
life has passed you by.
Both you and I need to roll the dice
and gamble on each other.

Once Upon A Time

Pine cone fights
little league tryouts
and biking in the woods.
Saturdays spent fishing (even if school was in).
Our feet splashing in the creek
as late as December most years.
Worries, oh worries,
sure there were—if USC would win
and on Sunday could get the keys to the gym?
Whatever happened to the days
that never had an end?
Sometime between pine cone fights (no greenies!)
after school and now the fights became for keeps.
Between courts, careers and weekend kids,
the things we thought were glitter have turned out to
make us mostly bitter.
Sometimes it's like dancing without the music
and you just can't get the beat.
Time always moves so slow
like sitting in sixth grade on the last
school day and vacation never seems to come.
Still, you hope that the night's not as long
or as dark as it seems.
Hard work, chores, Mass on Sunday,
duty, honor and respect
and never an impure thought
was the magic ticket out.
But nothing's quite as sad or boring
as the wings of dreams looking back
to youth and wondering who was telling the truth.

Contradictions — The Last Poem

How fashionably sad my poems are,
staring violently the black type thunders, weeps
and screams the emotions
of weekend mornings sprawled
in some bedroom in the evening half light.
The bold shyness speaking in crippled meter.
My, how they paralyze the present.

How despondently glad these scratchings
now walking the street on their own to find
a religious whore who believes 'tis better to give than
      receive.
Their vanity holding tightly to times
that like the want ads are still as empty as
the last pair of eyes that I believed.

Amazing, these relics which cling inside
like a cushion against the street,
their pages subject to decay like most guarded things.
Nostalgia has no finer taste when aged like wine
and change brings things new in time.
They are now children on their own
speaking, giving and taking alone on their merit.
For the most part they remain in their vault
unless tickled by familiar sound or scent.
No more writing, no more will I disturb their slumber
and no more will they stir mine.